THE HOW AND WHY
ACTIVITY WONDER® BOOK OF
THE HUMAN BODY

Written by Q. L. Pearce
Illustrated by Lesley Boney

Reviewed and Endorsed by:

William J. Pearce Ph.D.
Asst. Professor of Physiology
Loma Linda University
Loma Linda, CA

Director of Research
White Memorial Medical Center
Los Angeles, CA

Copyright © 1986 by RGA Publishing Group, Inc.
Illustrations Copyright © 1986 by Lesley Boney
Created by RGA Publishing Group
Published by Price/Stern/Sloan Publishers, Inc.
410 North La Cienega Boulevard, Los Angeles, California 90048

ISBN: 0-8431-4281-2

PRICE/STERN/SLOAN
Publishers, Inc., Los Angeles
1986

Have you ever thought about how amazing your body is? Of all the creatures who have ever lived, human beings have been able to make use of the earth and skies in more ways than any other animal. We can dive under the ocean...

Without even thinking about it, our heart beats, we digest our food, we breathe and our body heals and protects itself. But other animals do that, too. What makes us special? For one thing, we are capable of a wider range of movement than most animals. The human hand in particular can do anything from grasping a hammer to playing the piano. Another reason we are special is our brain. It is so highly evolved that we have been able to think about other things besides the need to survive on a day-to-day basis. We have developed a culture that includes language, science and art. What we learn, we pass on in books so that each generation adds to our knowledge.

fly through the air...

and even walk on the moon.

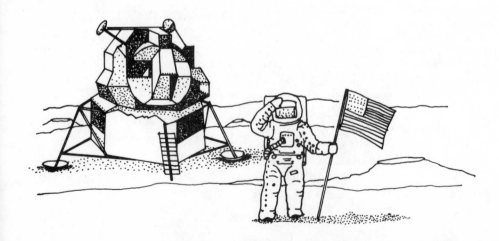

THE **HOW AND WHY** *Activity* WONDER® BOOK OF
THE HUMAN BODY

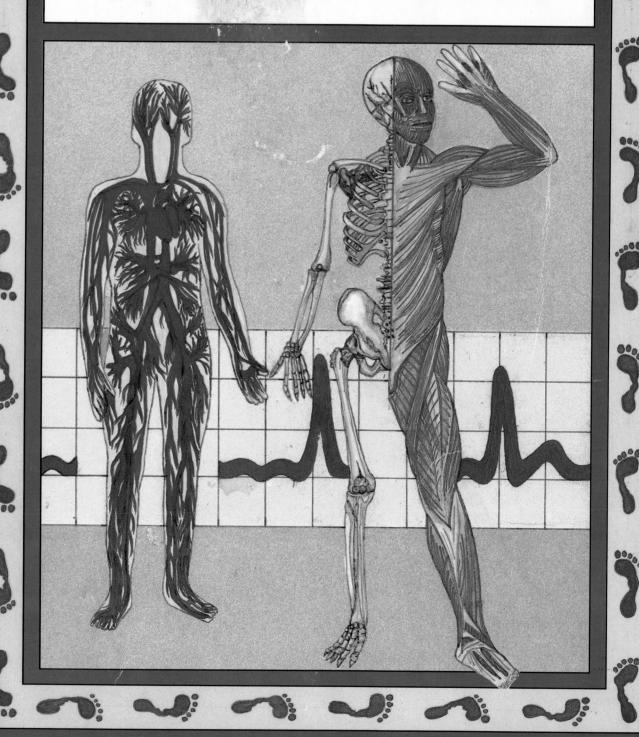

Moving around a lot helps to keep you warm when the weather is cold. That is what your muscles are doing when you shiver. They are moving as fast as they can to help you keep warm.

In the course of your lifetime you will grow over twenty-five feet of hair from your scalp.

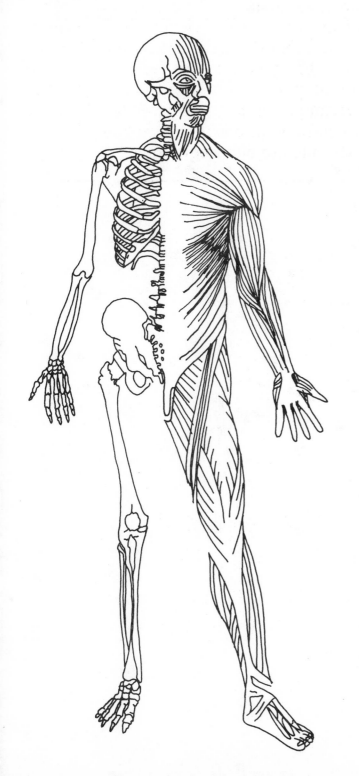

There are 656 muscles in the body. Over 200 of them are involved when you take one step.

All together, the veins, arteries and capillaries of the circulatory system measure over 62,000 miles.

We breathe about 3300 gallons of air each day.

When you are hungry your stomach muscles contract. If there is air in your stomach, this contraction will make a rumbling or growling sound.

The human body contains enough carbon to make the lead for 9000 pencils.

A single, red blood cell lives for about three months and makes about 130,000 round trips through the body.

Your skin completely replaces itself about once every month.

The most sensitive part of your body is your tongue. The least sensitive is the middle of your back.

The human body is approximately 70% water.

When you are breathing normally, your breath is released (or you exhale) at about 4 miles per hour. When you sneeze, it is as strong as a hurricane.

Many animals are faster than humans in a short run, but humans have more endurance and can outrun any other creature over long distances.

Your skull is not one piece. It is made up of 26 different bones.

The Cell

Every time we move or think, millions of tiny cells go to work. Each of us has over 50 trillion cells. (There are 500 times more cells in our bodies than there are stars in the galaxy!) Many cells are so tiny that 100,000 would fit on the head of a pin.

Others, like certain nerve cells, run the whole length of your leg. These cells work together like people in a big city. Some handle the food, some handle emergencies and some keep things clean. Still others help to communicate and make decisions. The scientists who study how they all work are called *physiologists* (fizz-ee-OL-o-jists).

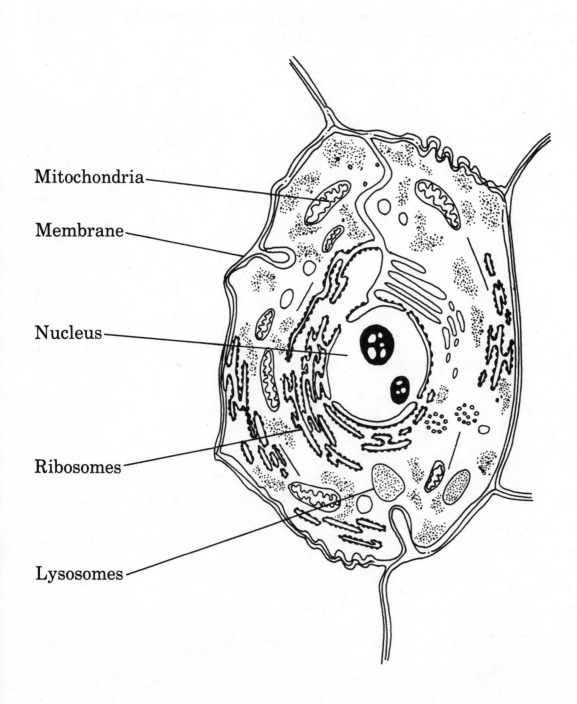

Mitochondria

Membrane

Nucleus

Ribosomes

Lysosomes

Genes

In the same way that an apple is protected by the peel, the cell and all of its parts are protected by a thick layer of fat called the *membrane*.

Your cells are constantly dying and being replaced. In the time it takes you to read this sentence, your body will have replaced over 50 million cells. The way you look has a lot to do with your cells. In each cell there are long "strings" called *genes* (jeens) which have information from both your mother's and father's genes. The cells "read" this information which tells them everything from how to make more cells to what color eyes you will have. This is why we often look something like our parents.

Genes affect the color of your eyes and hair and they decide how tall you will be. Can you match these parents with their children?

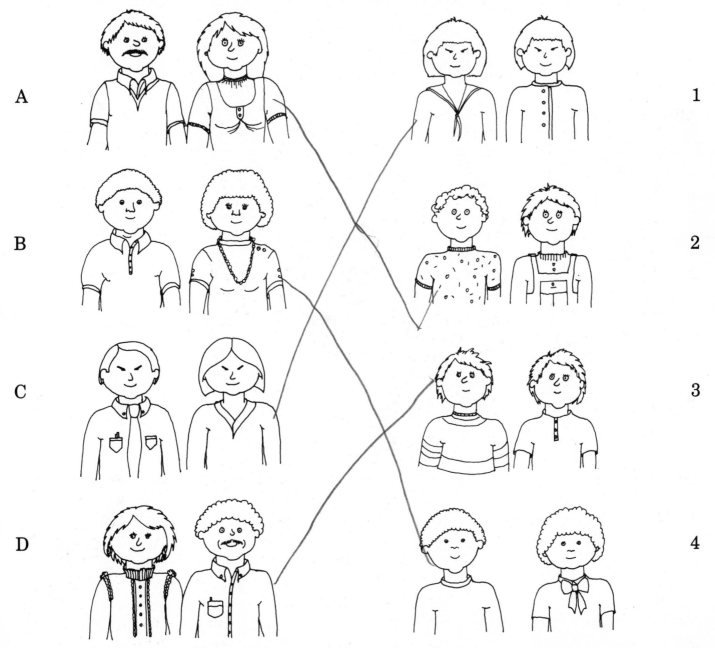

A
B
C
D

1
2
3
4

Blood

Different kinds of cells do different jobs. The job of the *red blood cell* is to carry *oxygen* to all the other cells in the body and to take *carbon dioxide* away. These cells are filled with *hemoglobin* (HEE-mo-glow-bin) which gives them their red color. There are also *white blood cells* that are like soldiers protecting the supply line.

When they find a particle or *bacterium* (bak-TEER-ee-um) that may cause disease, they flow around it and eat it up. Finally there are tiny cells called *platelets*. Their job is to make blood thicken or *clot* to stop the bleeding when you get a cut or scrape. These cells float in a thick fluid, much like sea water, called *plasma* (PLAZ-ma). All together these parts make up the *blood* which is pumped through a long network of tubes or blood vessels.

This white blood cell has spotted a harmful bacterium. Can you help the cell reach the bacterium through the maze?

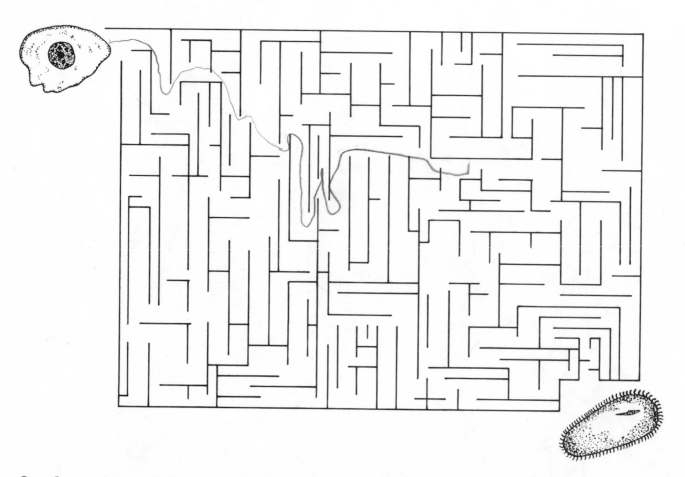

On the average 8% of your body weight is blood. So if you weigh 100 lbs. you have 8 pints of blood.

The Circulatory System

The blood is pumped by a very powerful muscle...the *heart*. When it contracts or squeezes, it forces the blood through a valve into large vessels called *arteries* (AR-ter-eez), and through them to all parts of the body. In the smallest blood vessels, *capillaries* (KAP-i-lar-eez), the blood drops off its supplies of fuel and oxygen, and picks up waste. The blood then travels back to the heart through vessels called *veins* (vanes).

If we think of our body as a city, then the circulatory system would be the subway train that travels through it. The heart sends the blood on hundreds of round trips every day, each trip taking less than a minute. Every time the heart beats, it is sending another wave of blood through the body. When you are resting, it beats approximately 70 times per minute. When you are working hard it can beat twice as fast.

How many words can you find in the word "capillaries"?

_____   _____

_____   _____

_____   _____

_____   _____

_____   _____

_____   _____

_____   _____

_____   _____

_____   _____

_____   _____

_____   _____

_____   _____

_____   _____

_____

— Aorta

— Pulmonary Artery

— Pulmonary Veins

— Atrium

— Ventricle

Why do you think your heart beats faster when you work hard?

7

The Lungs

How does oxygen get into the blood? When we breathe or inhale air through our mouth or nose it travels down a long tube in the throat called the *trachea* (TRAY-kee-uh), or "windpipe". The trachea divides into two parts called *bronchial* (BRONK-ee-al) tubes and each tube enters a lung. Once inside the lungs, the tubes divide like the branches of a tree. At the end of each tiny branch are many balloon-like clusters. These are the *alveoli* (AL-VEE-o-lie). There are so many of them that if they were flattened out, they would cover half of a tennis court. These little balloons are where the blood cells pick up their supply of oxygen, and drop off carbon dioxide waste which the body will not use.

You know all the words on this list. Can you find their proper place in the crosspatch?

3 letter words	4 letter words	5 letter words	6 letter words	7 letter words
Two	Nose	Blood	Throat	Trachea
Red	Tube	Lungs	Oxygen	Alveoli
	Cell	Mouth	Inhale	
	Pump			

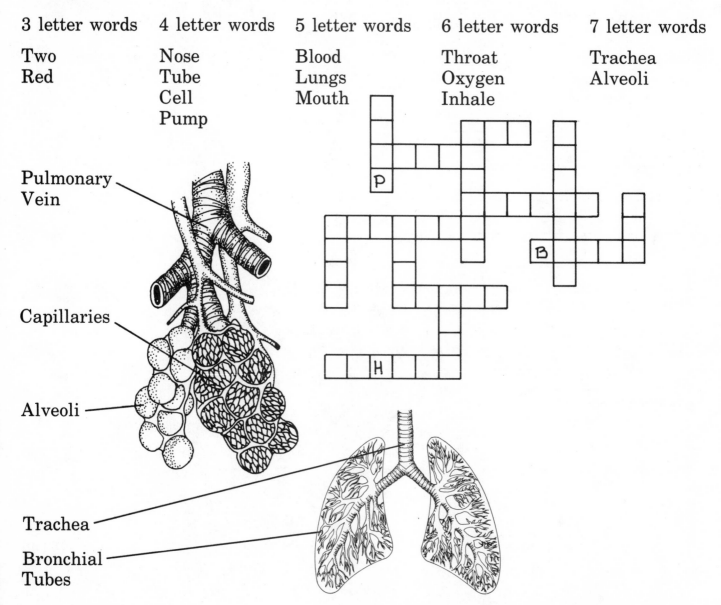

Pulmonary Vein

Capillaries

Alveoli

Trachea

Bronchial Tubes

How do you think the body eliminates the carbon dioxide from the lungs?

The Digestive System

The *alimentary canal* and two large glands, the *liver* and the *pancreas,* make up the *digestive system.* Fuel for our bodies is made from the food we eat. During your lifetime, you will eat about 60 thousand pounds of food. That's equal to the weight of six elephants. All of that food must be broken down so that it can be absorbed by the bloodstream. The process begins at the top of the alimentary canal, the *mouth,* and ends at the bottom, the *rectum.* The canal is about thirty feet long, all curled and tucked inside you. First, the food is chewed and mixed with saliva. Your tongue pushes the food down the *esophagus* (ee-SOFF-uh-gus) and into the *stomach* which mixes it with digestive juices to break it down even more. Then it travels into the *small intestine.* Here it is digested enough to be absorbed and passed into the capillaries. Next it enters the blood stream to be carried to all parts of the body. The material that is not used enters the *large intestine,* where the water is reabsorbed. Everything else accumulates in the rectum and is eliminated through the *anus.*

Unscramble the letters to discover parts of the digestive system and write the answers on the drawing to the right.

A. HPSOAGEUS =

B. UHTMO =

C. LMALS TSETENIIN =

D. GRALE NITENIEST =

E. HAMCOST =

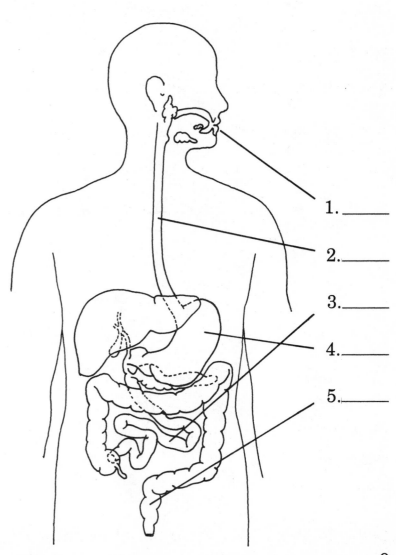

1.____

2.____

3.____

4.____

5.____

9

The Pancreas

The digestive juices which are used in the small intestine come from the *pancreas* (PAN-kree-us). These juices contain special proteins called *enzymes* (EN-zimz). The enzymes break food down into small enough particles to be absorbed into the blood stream. Besides enzymes, the pancreas makes chemicals called *hormones*. The most important one is *insulin* (IN-soo-lin) which controls how much sugar is in the blood. Another name for this sugar is *glucose* (GLOO-kose). Glucose is fuel for many of the body's cells, particularly those in the brain.

Can you complete these sentences about the pancreas?

Enzymes are a kind of _ _ _ _ _ _ _

Insulin controls _ _ _ _ _ in the blood

_ _ _ _ _ _ _ is a hormone

Glucose is a fuel for _ _ _ _ _ _ _

The pancreas produces _ _ _ _ _ _ _ _

It also produces _ _ _ _ _ _ _

The blood _ _ _ _ _ _ absorbs food particles

_ _ _ _ _ _ _ is a form of sugar

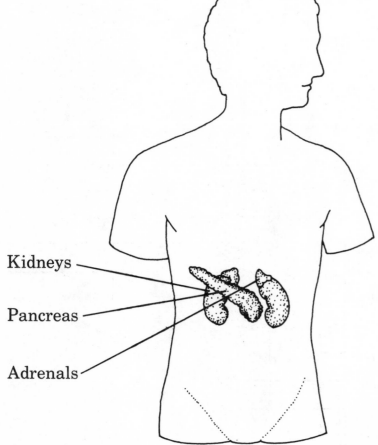

Kidneys

Pancreas

Adrenals

The Liver

Once the food has been absorbed into the bloodstream, the blood enters the *liver*. The liver makes poisons in the food (like alcohol or food additives) less harmful through chemical reactions. It also controls protein levels. Although it only weighs about 3 pounds, scientists have counted 500 different jobs that the liver does. If the tubes of the liver were laid end to end they would stretch 60 miles.

Deep inside the liver is the *gall bladder*. This produces a soap-like fluid called *bile*, which is used by the small intestine to help digest fat.

Solve the code and use it to fill in the puzzle.

A	= 1 + 2 =
B	= 2 + 7 =
C	= 3 + 3 =
D	= 6 + 4 =
E	= 12 + 3 =
F	= 4 + 16 =
G	= 7 + 1 =
H	= 5 + 9 =
I	= 9 + 9 =
J	= 21 + 3 =
K	= 9 + 7 =
L	= 12 + 14 =
M	= 2 + 2 =
N	= 10 + 9 =
O	= 2 + 3 =
P	= 14 + 11 =

Q	= 5 + 6 =
R	= 18 + 18 =
S	= 10 + 20 =
T	= 5 + 2 =
U	= 19 + 8 =
V	= 11 + 11 =
W	= 23 + 6 =
X	= 4 + 24 =
Y	= 18 + 5 =
Z	= 5 + 76 =

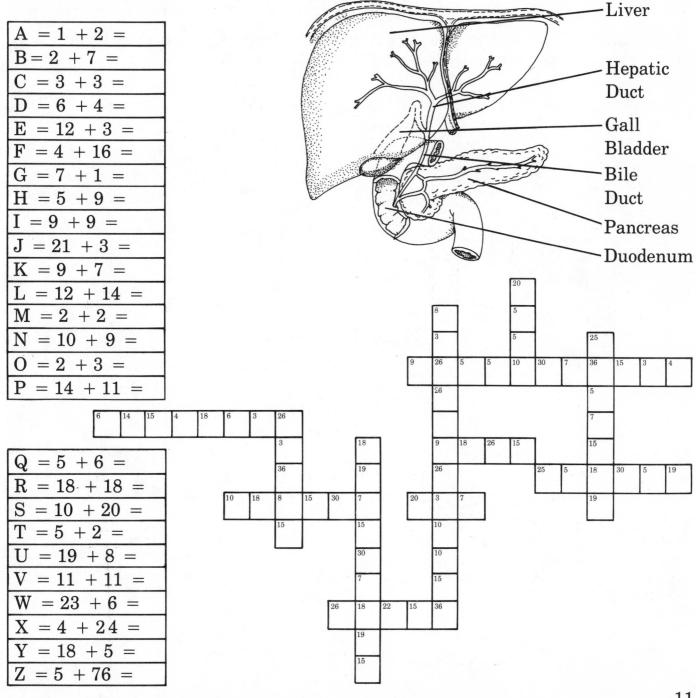

Liver

Hepatic Duct

Gall Bladder

Bile Duct

Pancreas

Duodenum

The Kidneys

There is another organ that protects our body from harmful poisons. We even have two of them. They are the *kidneys* (KIDneez). Kidney cells are like tiny filters. As the blood flows through the kidney, blood cells are too large to fit through the filter so they continue on their trip back to the heart. Some of the fluid and chemicals *do* squeeze through, and they flow into a special tube that is something like a conveyor belt. As this fluid is moved along, the kidney reabsorbs the water and important chemicals that the body needs. The rest, liquid wastes and poisons, are left behind. They travel to the bladder and are later released as *urine.* We only have about 2½ gallons of blood, and it must be filtered each time it circulates through the body. The kidneys filter and "clean" about 50 gallons of fluid from the blood every day.

There are many looping tubes inside the kidney. Can you find your way through this amazing loop?

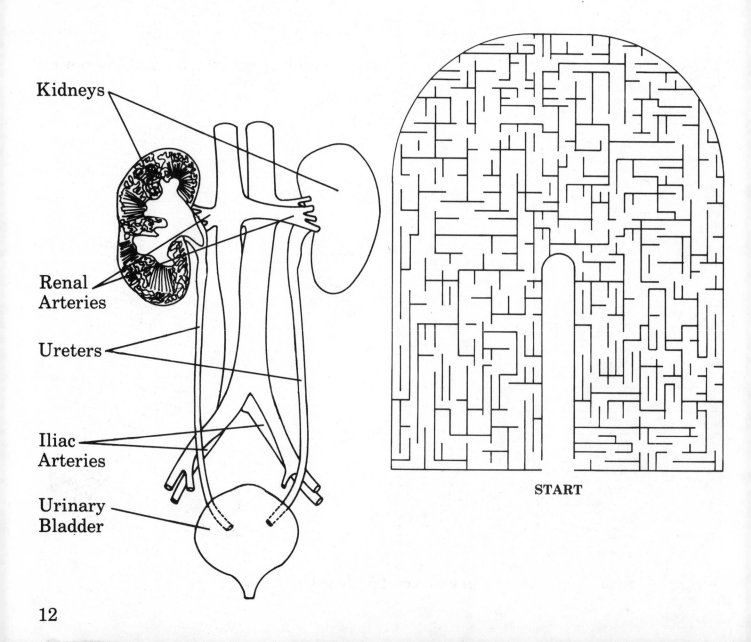

Kidneys

Renal Arteries

Ureters

Iliac Arteries

Urinary Bladder

START

The Nervous System

All of the organs and systems in the body work without your having to think about it because of the *nervous system*. This is the body's communication and control center. It is made up of 14 billion cells called *neurons* (NOOR-onz). The cells work by sending tiny chemical signals from one to another. It is sort of like passing news along a line of people. The signals eventually reach the *brain* which sends a message back, telling the body what to do.

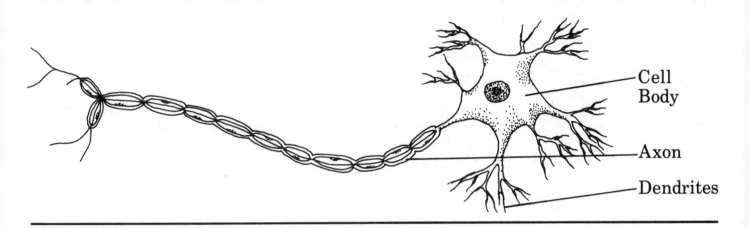

Cell Body

Axon

Dendrites

Follow the pathways to see which messages from the brain are reaching which parts of the body.

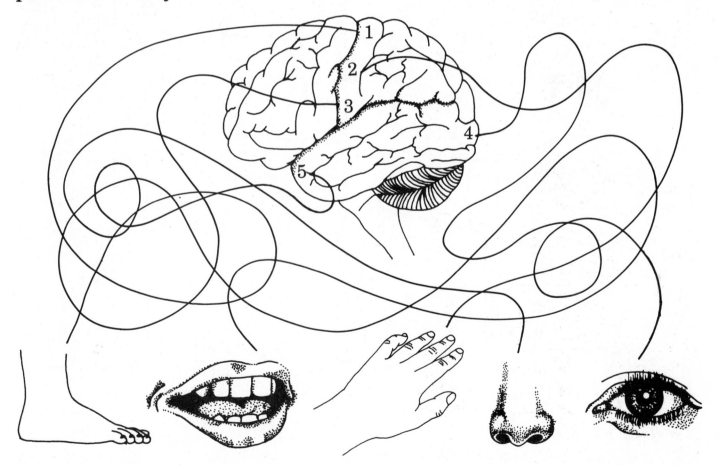

When do you think your nerves are the least active?

The Nervous System

The *brain* is the center of the nervous system. It controls all of the body's activities, both *autonomic,* such as breathing, blood circulation and digestion, and *voluntary,* such as movement, speech and thought. It does all of this, yet weighs only about three pounds. The brain has three main sections. The *cerebrum* (se-REE-brum) is the largest and is divided into right and left hemispheres. In humans the cerebrum is highly developed, enabling us to think, learn, understand and reason. The *cerebellum* (ser-uh-BELL-um) has two hemispheres also. It is responsible for all voluntary muscular coordination. The autonomic functions, like the beating of the heart and breathing, are controlled by the *medulla* (meh-DOO-lah). It is about the size of your thumb and is at the beginning of the *spinal cord,* which, with the *brain,* makes up the *central nervous system.*

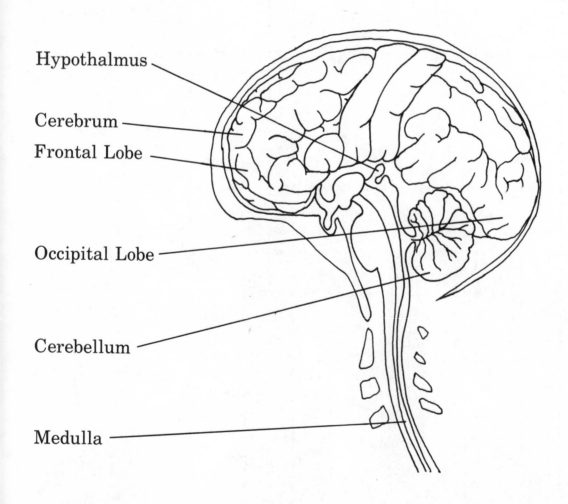

Hypothalmus

Cerebrum

Frontal Lobe

Occipital Lobe

Cerebellum

Medulla

The Spinal Cord

The spinal cord is a thick bundle of nerve fibers with a tough protective covering. It extends four-fifths of the way down the back, inside the *spinal column,* which is a hollow chain of bones called *vertebrae* (VER-tuh-bray). Every part of the body is connected to the central nervous system by 43 pairs of nerves. Each pair is like a two lane highway with impulses traveling in one direction in one nerve and back again in the other nerve. 31 pairs of nerves connect to the spinal cord and 12 pairs go to and from the brain by way of the medulla. These nerves crisscross at the medulla so that the right side of the body is controlled by the left side of the brain and vice versa.

See if you can find these words from the story hidden in the puzzle below.

Spinal	Vertebrae	Nerve
Fibers	Chain	Body
Impulses	Brain	Pairs
Left	Bundle	Hollow
Medulla	Signal	Protective
Central	Cord	Thick
Right	Bone	

L	W	O	L	L	O	H	W	J	P	R	I
E	T	E	B	P	E	A	U	Y	Y	I	I
A	B	R	A	I	N	F	D	K	U	G	M
H	Q	I	M	R	O	O	N	T	M	H	P
V	R	S	R	E	B	I	F	E	M	T	U
S	E	I	J	O	A	E	D	H	R	U	L
K	L	G	K	H	L	U	T	R	H	V	S
C	D	N	C	Q	L	E	T	R	O	Y	E
I	N	A	A	L	A	R	T	N	E	C	S
H	U	L	A	N	I	P	S	A	U	V	H
T	B	E	V	I	T	C	E	T	O	R	P

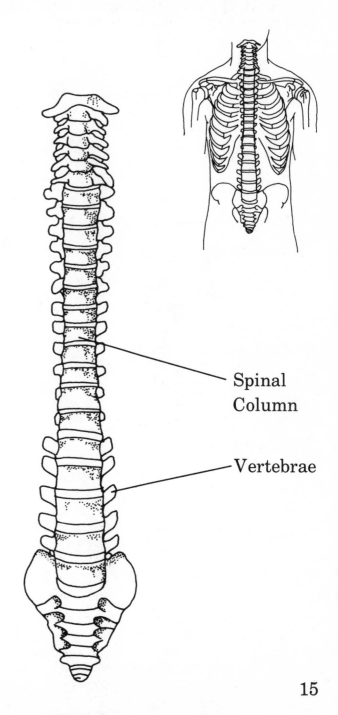

Spinal Column

Vertebrae

15

The nervous system also has a network of nerves outside the spinal column. *Sensory* nerves carry messages from the sense organs (eyes, ears, nose, tongue and fingers) to the brain. The *motor* nerves then carry the orders from the brain to muscles or glands. Some messages travel as fast as 250 miles per hour. The body also has an automatic system called *reflexes*. If you touch something very hot you jerk your hand away without thinking about it. That is because the message takes a short cut through the spinal cord called a *reflex arc*. The original impulse still travels to the brain, where it will be felt as pain, but the spinal cord automatically sends a command to the muscles in your arm to pull your hand away.

Fill in the answers to the questions below, then write each letter above the line with the same number. You will find a part of the body that has no nerves.

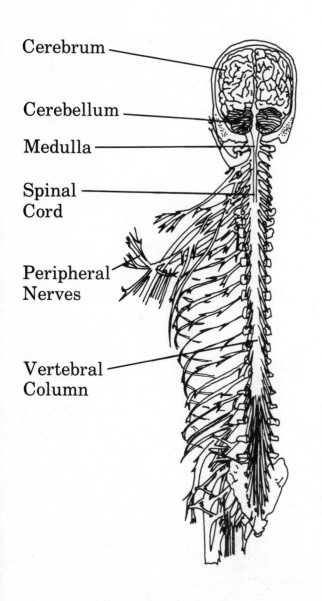

Cerebrum

Cerebellum

Medulla

Spinal Cord

Peripheral Nerves

Vertebral Column

A. An automatic nerve reaction:

$\overline{}\ \overline{}\ \overline{}\ \overline{}\ \overline{}\ \overline{}$
7 3 11 16 3 14

B. Nerves that carry messages from the sense organs:

$\overline{}\ \overline{}\ \overline{}\ \overline{}\ \overline{}\ \overline{}\ \overline{}$
12 3 9 12 2 8 17

C. Another name for the backbone:

$\overline{}\ \overline{}\ \overline{}\ \overline{}\ \overline{}\ \overline{}\ \overline{}\ \overline{}\ \overline{}\ \overline{}\ \overline{}\ \overline{}$
12 5 1 9 4 16 20 2 16 15 17 9

D. Motor nerves carry orders to muscles and:

$\overline{}\ \overline{}\ \overline{}\ \overline{}\ \overline{}\ \overline{}$
6 16 4 9 18 12

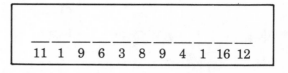

11 1 9 6 3 8 9 4 1 16 12

Can you think of another part of your body that doesn't have nerves?

The Senses: Sight

The nervous system gets its information from *sensory organs* that tell us about the world around us through the five senses of *sight, hearing, smell, taste* and *touch*. The *eye* is the organ of sight. It is a small round ball with a tough white covering. In the front is a transparent circular patch, the *cornea*. It's like a curved window filled with clear liquid. Behind that is a colored tissue or *iris* with a hole in it called the *pupil*. A series of tiny muscles in the eye expand or contract the pupil depending on the amount of light falling on the eye. The light travels through the *lens* to the inside of the eye where it excites nerve endings in the lining or *retina*.

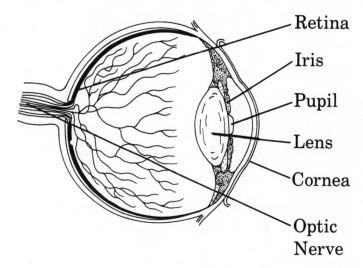

These tiny nerve endings connect to the *optic nerve* which sends a picture to the brain.

Use your eyes to find the 11 mistakes in this picture.

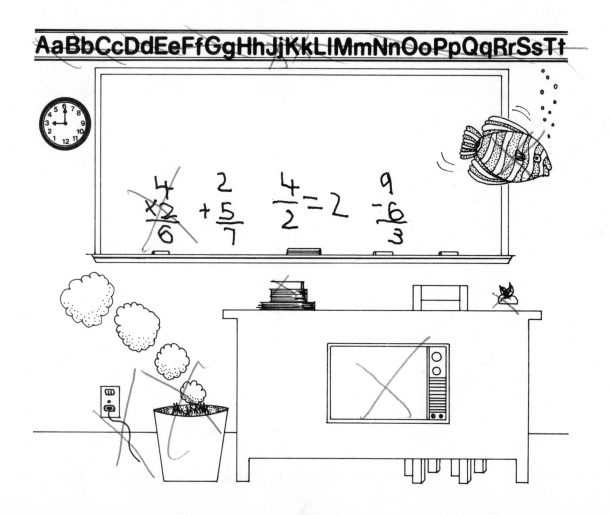

The Senses: Hearing

The organ of hearing is the *ear*. Sound waves enter the ear and strike a membrane called the *eardrum* which passes the vibration to three tiny bones. These bones are commonly known as the *hammer, anvil* and *stirrup* because their shapes resemble these objects. The vibration continues into a special organ that is filled with liquid and is lined with *auditory nerves* connected to the brain. Also in the ear are the fluid-filled *semicircular canals*. They sense the effect of gravity on the fluid and send this information to the brain so that it can keep the body in balance. Sometimes these signals can be a little confusing, like when you are on a rocking boat. That is the reason for the dizzy, uncomfortable feeling knows as sea sickness.

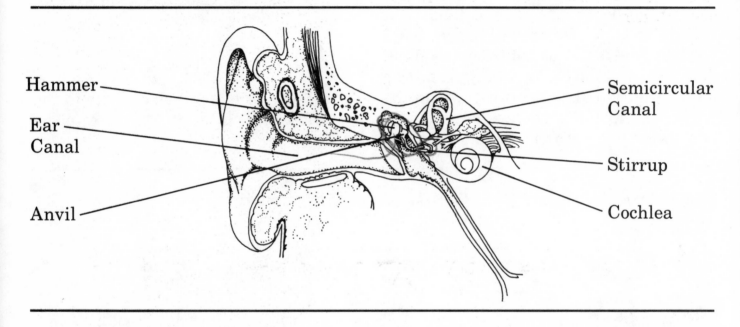

Hammer — Ear Canal — Anvil — Semicircular Canal — Stirrup — Cochlea

Can you find the path through the maze that the sound will travel from one boy to the other?

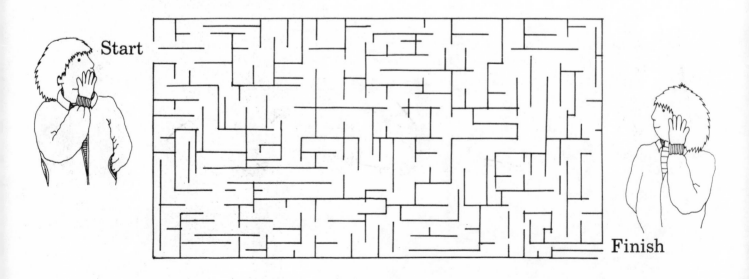

Start

Finish

The Senses: Smell

The nose has nerves that tell the brain what we are smelling. Although the sense of smell is not as highly developed in humans as in other animals, most people can identify at least 4000 different smells. This is done through nerve endings or *receptors* that line the inside of the nose. Before an odor can be detected, it must mix with the *mucus* in the nose which causes a chemical reaction that stimulates the *olefactory nerves*. The sense of smell is the most common of the senses in the animal kingdom. It is the first of the senses to develop in a newborn baby and it is the first one we lose.

There are all different kinds and shapes of noses. Can you find the two that are alike?

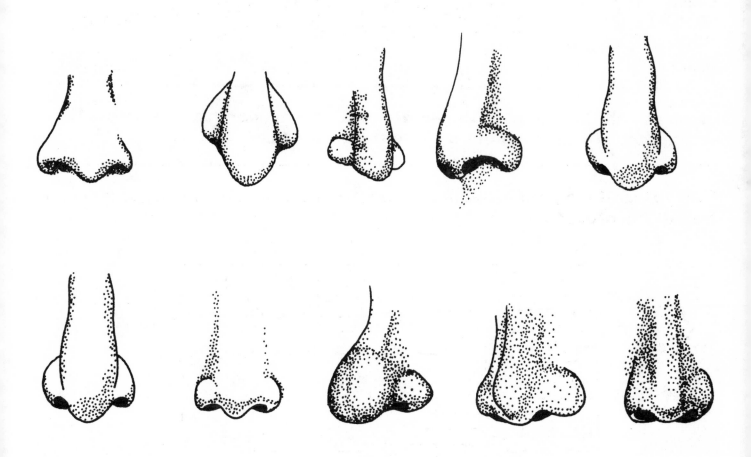

Your sense of smell gets better when you are hungry. Can you think of something that may make it less sensitive?

The Senses: Taste

When we put something in our mouths, it is exposed to tiny receptors in our *taste buds*. There are about 10,000 taste buds. Most of them are on the surface of the tongue, but some are on the roof of the mouth, or *palate* (PAL-et), and some are in the throat. We recognize four different kinds of tastes — sweet, bitter, sour, and salty. Each one is sensed by a different part of the tongue. Bitterness is sensed on the side, sourness near the base, sweetness at the tip.

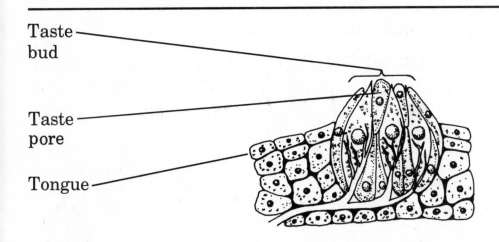

Taste bud

Taste pore

Tongue

Cross out all the letters in the puzzle that appear more than 3 times. The letters that are left spell out a sense that helps taste to work.

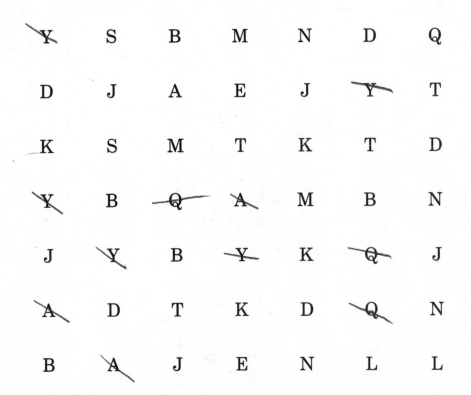

Y S B M N D Q

D J A E J Y T

K S M T K T D

Y B Q A M B N

J Y B Y K Q J

A D T K D Q N

B A J E N L L

The Senses: Touch

The sense of touch includes five sensations — touch, pain, pressure, hot and cold. These are recognized by special nerve endings, mostly in the skin cells, that send messages to the brain. Not all parts of the body are equally sensitive. Some areas such as the tips of the fingers have hundreds of receptors which make them very sensitive. Other parts, like hair and fingernails, have no receptors at all. Some areas have only a few receptors so the messages they send to the brain are hard to interpret. Your heart has very few receptors. If someone's heart hurts, the pain may actually feel as if it is coming from his left arm. This is called *referred pain*.

Can you avoid all of the unpleasant sensations in this maze to reach the sunny meadow?

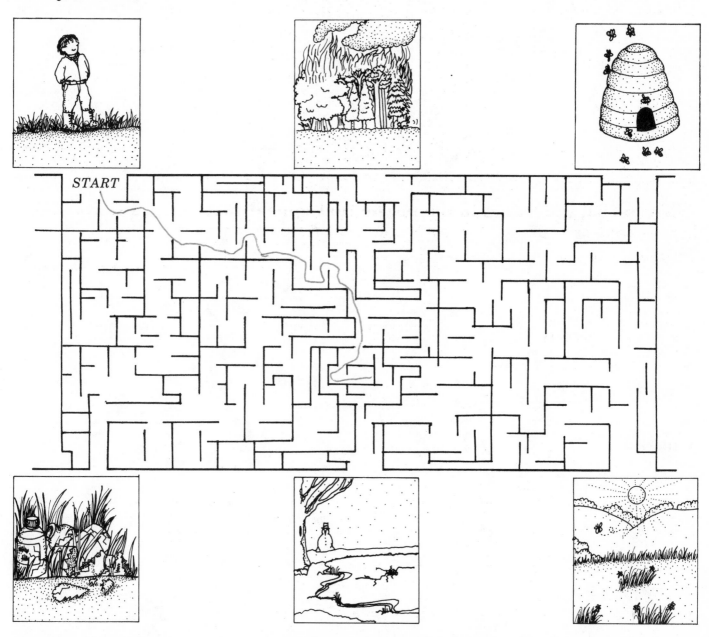

START

Why do you think it is important that we feel things like heat, cold and pain?

Glands

The senses bring information to the brain. When it decides what to do, the brain sends instructions to the muscles or *glands*. The glands release special chemicals called *hormones* into the blood. They control things like how you grow, and when you get hungry or sleepy. One of the many jobs of the *hypothalmus,* a gland in the brain, is to sense when the water level in your body is too low. It sends a signal to the brain to make you feel thirsty. The hypothalmus also stimulates the *pituitary gland* to work. The pituitary produces hormones that cause you to grow and it also stimulates other glands, like the *thyroid.* This gland helps to produce energy from food. There are many kinds of glands in the body and each one has special jobs to do.

How many words can you make from the word "pituitary"?

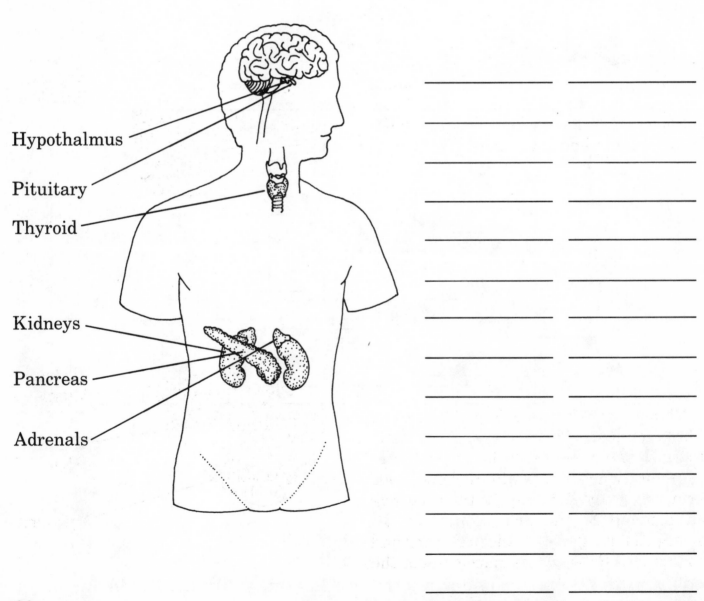

Hypothalmus

Pituitary

Thyroid

Kidneys

Pancreas

Adrenals

Muscular System

We can move because of our *muscles*. There are three kinds.

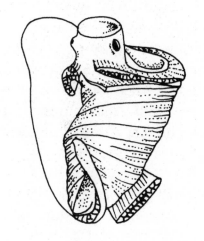

Cardiac Muscle

Cardiac (KAR-dee-ak) muscles are found in the heart.

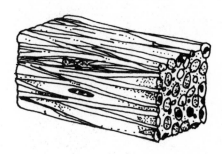

Smooth Muscle

Smooth muscles are found mainly in the blood vessels and intestines.

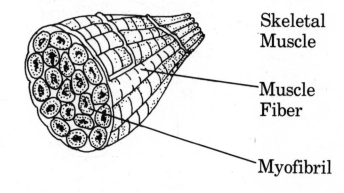

Skeletal Muscle

Muscle Fiber

Myofibril

Skeletal muscles are long bundles of fibres connected to our bones. They come in pairs and can only pull, not push. For example, when you want to bend your arm, the *bicep* (BUY-sep), a thick muscle on the top of the arm, contracts. To straighten it again, the bicep relaxes and the *tricep* (TRY-sep), the muscle under the arm, contracts.

The Skeletal System

The *skeleton* is a framework of bones that holds our body up and gives it its shape. It is made of 206 bones. There are three types of bones; *long bones,* like those in your arms and legs with thick ends that fit into other bones, *short bones* like those in the wrist, and *flat bones* such as the *ribs.* Bones like the *skull, ribs,* and *spinal column* protect the softer organs inside from damage. All bones have a hard outer surface made mostly from the minerals *calcium* and *phosphorus.* Inside is the spongy *marrow,* made of fat cells. The marrow of certain bones is where blood cells are produced. *Ligaments* hold bones together at the joints.

There are 10 bones missing from this skeleton. Can you fill them in?

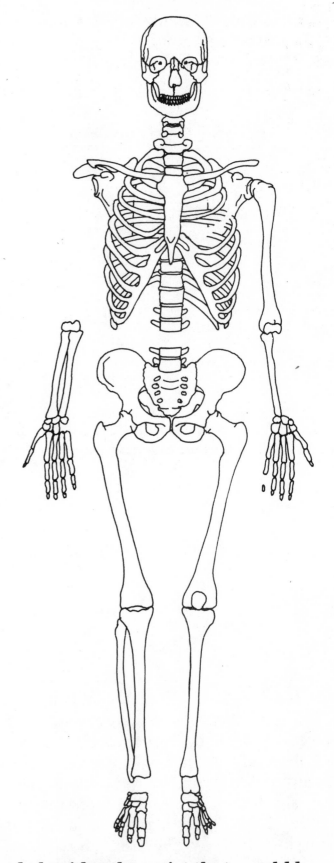

Can you think of another place in the body besides the wrist that would have short bones?

Joints

The *joints* are where bones meet. They are the reason you can bend your arms and legs. Try to walk or pick something up without bending your knees or elbows. You will see how important our joints are. Some joints, like those for our ribs or those in the skull, don't move at all. They grow together to form a hard protective covering for the delicate organs inside.

Hip
Joint

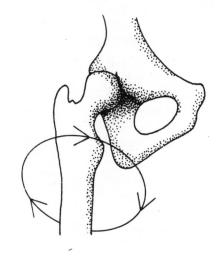

Elbow
Joint

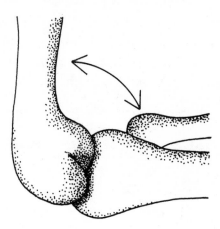

Can you fill in the correct answers to the questions about your skeleton?

The _ _ _ _ are not made to move.

The joints in the _ _ _ _ _ do not move either.

Solid joints _ _ _ _ _ _ _ the organs.

Bones are held together by _ _ _ _ _ _ _ _ _ .

Your _ _ _ _ _ joints move.

_ _ _ _ _ _ are where bones meet.

The skeleton is made of _ _ _ _ _ .

Your arms and legs _ _ _ _ because of joints.

The Skin

The body needs a covering to keep it from drying out and to protect it. The *skin* gives our body a flexible, air tight, waterproof shield. It also helps to regulate body temperature. When it is cold, the blood vessels in the skin contract. When it is too hot, the vessels expand bringing more blood to the surface where it loses heat. To help lose the extra heat, the skin releases fluid through the sweat glands which cools through evaporation. An average person doing light work can lose up to a quart of fluid a day from the openings of *pores* of more than 2 million sweat glands.

The skin is made of two main layers. The inner layer, or *dermis,* contains capillaries, nerve endings, sweat glands, tiny erector muscles and the roots of hairs. The outer layer, or *epidermis,* is formed by dead cells that are constantly replaced from underneath. We wash or rub millions of epidermal cells from our skin every day.

Use what you've learned about the skin to solve this puzzle

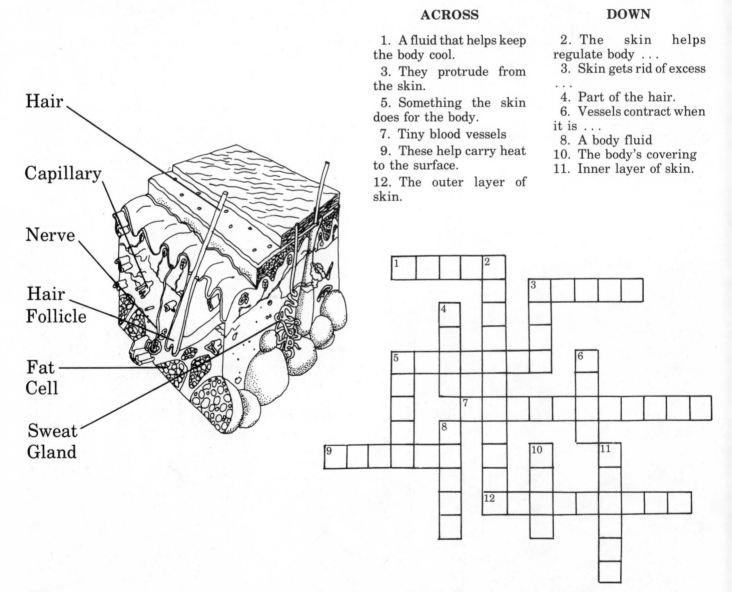

Hair

Capillary

Nerve

Hair Follicle

Fat Cell

Sweat Gland

ACROSS

1. A fluid that helps keep the body cool.
3. They protrude from the skin.
5. Something the skin does for the body.
7. Tiny blood vessels
9. These help carry heat to the surface.
12. The outer layer of skin.

DOWN

2. The skin helps regulate body . . .
3. Skin gets rid of excess . . .
4. Part of the hair.
6. Vessels contract when it is . . .
8. A body fluid
10. The body's covering
11. Inner layer of skin.

Reproduction

All living things must be able to reproduce themselves. In the human body, the process begins with single cells. In the female body are *egg* cells. The male body produces *sperm* cells. When these different cells come in contact with each other, the male cell must break through the wall of the egg to *fertilize* it. The egg and sperm combine to form one cell, which splits in-to two cells. These cells also split, and the process continues until there are thousands of cells. These are called an *em-bryo* (EM-bree-o). Tissues then begin to form and a tiny human begins to take shape. This development of the embryo takes place in the *uterus* (YOU-ter-us) of the female body over a period of nine months. At the end of that time, when con-ditions are just right, the muscles in the uterus contract to push the baby out and a child is born.

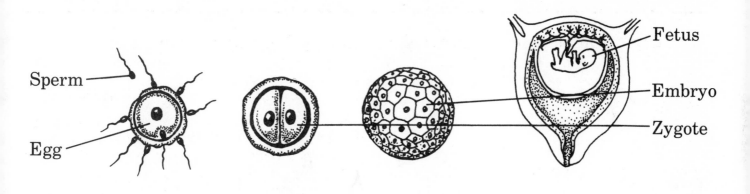

There are ten babies pictured below. Can you find the two that are exactly alike?

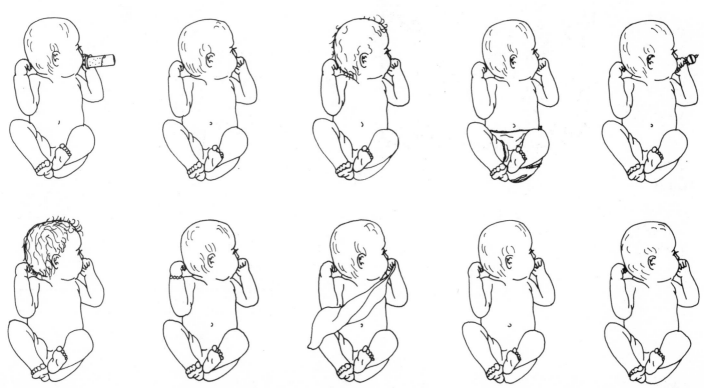

Nutrition

Your body is better than any machine because it improves with use. To keep it in proper working order, you must keep it clean, get plenty of rest and exercise and eat the right foods everyday. This includes something from each of the four main food groups. These groups are meat and poultry, fruits and vegetables, dairy products and breads and cereals. By eating many different kinds of foods, you can be sure that your body will get all the *vitamins* and *minerals* it needs. Take good care of your body, and give it what it needs. Remember, you want it to last a lifetime.

There are many words from the story hidden in this puzzle. Circle all of them that you can find.

Word List

Vegetables
Brain
Bones
Food
Fruit
Blood
Cereals
Minerals
Vitamins
Nerve
Dairy
Body
Meat
Exercise
Cells
Muscles
Skin
Energy
Rest
Eat
Breads
Poultry

```
E T H I E S K I N O S W L
T D A D R Q N F T L T J L
E S K M A I E I A G H P Y
V L E J A I M E M E A T D
E A Q R P O R O S A N R N
T K B J D E E Y M N T I A
S M U S C L E S S C F I V
U Q D S E L B A T E G E V
S A O M L N O L I F E L K
D D O O L B D X U V N I Y
A G F L S T Y B R L E S N
E S I C R E X E F L R W S
R S L A R E N I M I G Y I
B O Y R T L U O P B Y P R
V Y N Y L S O J B N B A K
```

Scientists still have a lot to learn about the human body but the best tools for finding the answers are the products of our own remarkable brain ... Curiosity, Reason and *Imagination!*

Can you identify these parts of the human body?
Draw a line showing where these parts of the body belong.

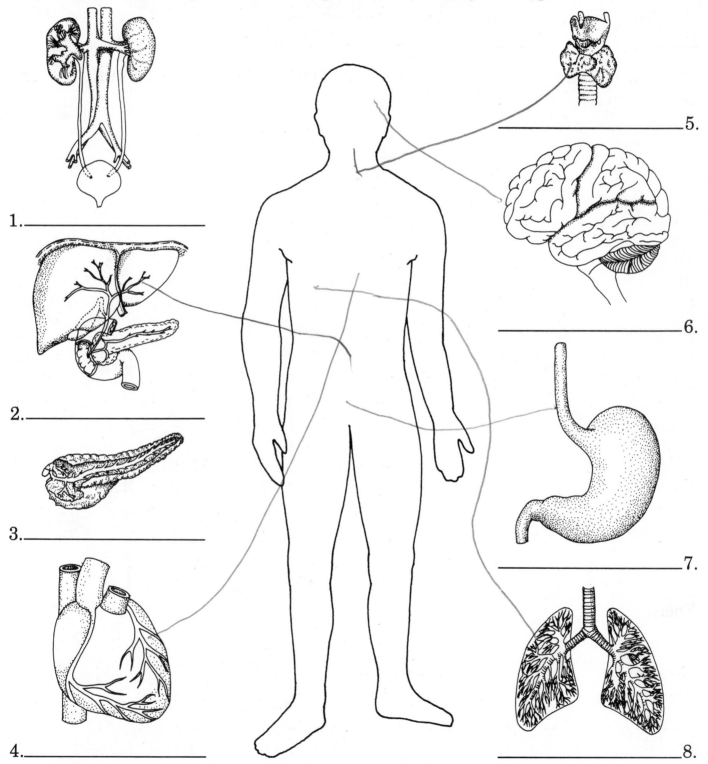

1._____

2._____

3._____

4._____

5._____

6._____

7._____

8._____

If you were building a robot, what human parts do you think it should have?

Answers

Page 5

A = 3   C = 1
B = 4   D = 2

Page 6

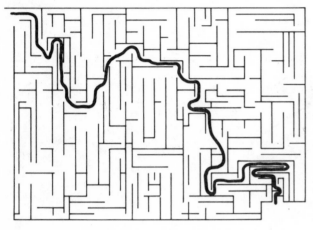

Page 7

Cap, Car, Call, Area, All, Ape, Pill, Par, Pal, Pale, Ill, Lap, Lip, Lisp, Liar, Rip, Rail, Pail, Pair, Sail, Slip, Sale, Spare, Spill, Place, Lace, Sip, Cape, Sap

Because your body needs more oxygen

Page 8

We exhale

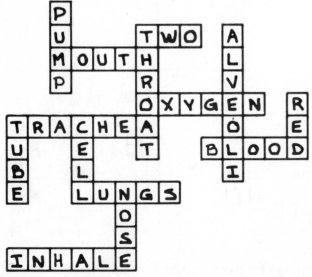

Page 9

A. = Esophagus #2
B. = Mouth #1
C. = Small Intestine #3
D. = Large Intestine #5
E. = Stomach #4

1. B   4. E
2. A   5. D
3. C

Page 10

Protein	Cells	Stream
Sugar	Hormones	Glucose
Insulin	Enzymes	

Page 11

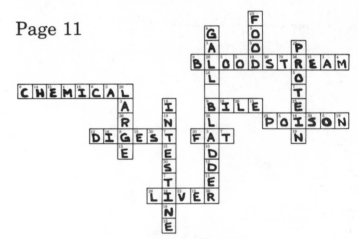

Page 12

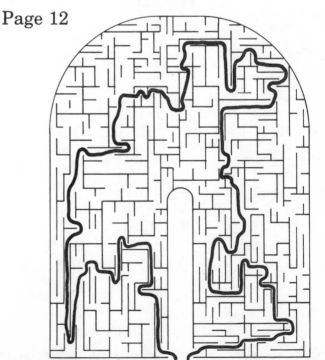

Page 13

When you sleep

Page 15

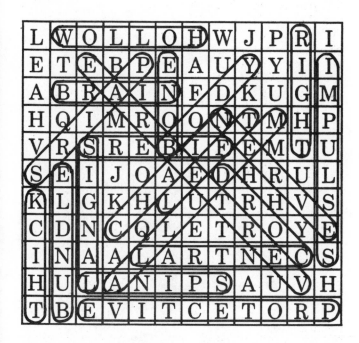

Page 16

Reflex
Sensory
Spinal Column
Glands
Fingernails

The hair doesn't have nerves either.

Page 17

Did You See...

Too many chair legs, half an apple missing, book without pages, T.V. in desk, trash on fire, incomplete alphabet, unconnected electric plug, 4x2 =6 is wrong, clock numbers are backward, fish swimming off blackboard and alphabet miss ing the I?

Page 18

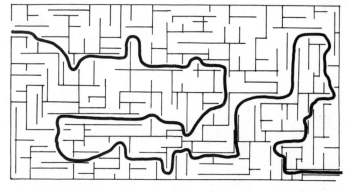

Page 19

A cold or smoking can lessen your sense of smell.

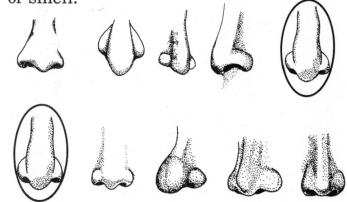

Page 20

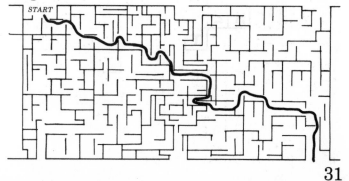

Page 21

Page 21

If we didn't feel these things we wouldn't know if we were in danger.

Page 22

Pit, Pry, Tar, Rat, Rip, Put, Pay, Lap, Play, Dig, Nap, Plan, Plug, Gap, Tag, Lip, Try, Tap, Ray, Pair, Rag, Tip

Page 24

The ankles have short bones.

Page 25

Ribs
Skull
Protect
Ligaments
Elbow
Joints
Bones
Bend

Page 26

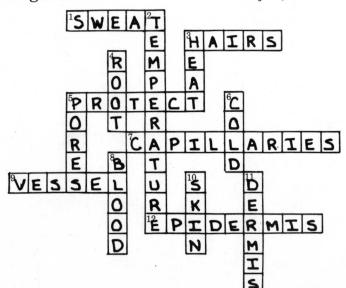

Page 27

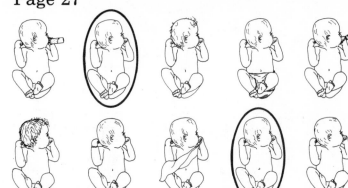

Page 28

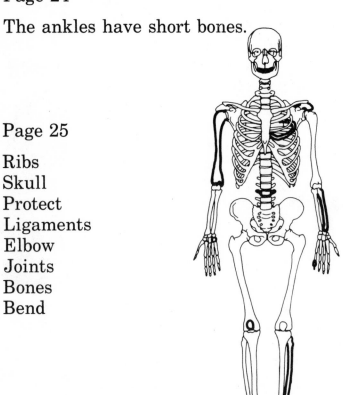

Page 29

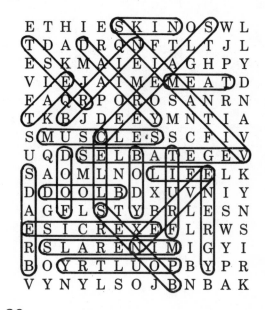

1. Kidneys
2. Liver
3. Pancreas
4. Heart
5. Thyroid
6. Brain
7. Stomach
8. Lungs